The
First Christmas
of
New England

Wassail.

The First Christmas of New England

of

New England

by

Harriet Beecher Stowe

APPLEWOOD BOOKS • BEDFORD, MASSACHUSETTS

The First Christmas of New England
was originally published in 1876.

Thank you for purchasing an Applewood Book.
Applewood reprints America's lively classics—
books from the past that are still of interest
to modern readers. For a free copy of our
current catalog, write to:
Applewood Books
P.O. Box 365
Bedford, MA 01730

ISBN 1-55709-479-9

Library of Congress Control Number: 2002110036

3 5 7 9 10 8 6 4 2

Printed in Mexico

Contents

Chapter I

The Arrival

T HE shores of the Atlantic coast of America may well be a terror to navigators. They present an inexorable wall, against which forbidding and angry waves incessantly dash, and around which shifting winds continually rave. The approaches to safe harbors are few in number, intricate and difficult, requiring the skill of practiced pilots.

But, as if with a pitying spirit of hospitality, old Cape Cod, breaking from the iron line of the coast, like a generous-hearted sailor intent on helpfulness, stretches an hundred miles outward, and, curving his sheltering arms in a protective circle, gives a noble harborage. Of this harbor of Cape Cod the report of our governmental Coast Survey thus speaks: "It is one of the finest harbors for ships of war on the whole of our Atlantic coast. The width and freedom from obstruction of every kind at its entrance and the extent of sea room upon the bay side make it accessible to vessels of the largest class in almost all winds. This advantage, its capacity, depth of water, excellent anchorage, and the complete shelter it affords from all winds, render it one of the most valuable ship harbors upon our coast."

We have been thus particular in our mention of this place, because here, in this harbor, opened the first scene in the most wonderful drama of modern history.

Let us look into the magic mirror of the past and see this harbor of Cape Cod on the morning of the 11th of November, in the year of our Lord 1620, as described to us in the simple words of the pilgrims: "A pleasant bay, circled round, except the entrance, which is about four miles over from land to land, *compassed about to the very sea* with oaks, pines, junipers, sassafras, and other sweet weeds. It is a harbor wherein a thousand sail of ship may safely ride."

Such are the woody shores of Cape Cod as we look back upon them in that distant November day, and the harbor lies like a great crystal gem on the bosom of a virgin wilderness. The "fir trees, the pine trees, and the bay," rejoice together in freedom, for as yet the axe has spared them; in the noble bay no shipping has found shelter; no voice or sound of civilized man has broken the sweet calm of the forest. The oak leaves, now turned to crimson and maroon by the autumn frosts, reflect themselves in flushes of color on the still waters. The golden leaves of the sassafras yet cling to the branches, though their life has passed, and every brushing wind bears showers of them down to the water. Here and there the dark spires of the cedar and the green leaves and red berries of the holly contrast with these lighter tints. The forest foliage grows down to the water's edge, so that the dash of the rising and falling tide washes into the shaggy cedar boughs which here and there lean over and dip in the waves.

No voice or sound from earth or sky proclaims that anything unwonted is coming or doing on these shores to-day. The wandering Indians, moving their hunting-camps along the woodland paths, saw no sign in the stars that morning, and no different color in the sunrise from what had been in the days of their fathers. Panther and wild-cat under their furry coats felt no thrill of coming dispossession, and saw nothing through their great golden eyes but the dawning of a day just like all other days—when "the sun ariseth and they gather themselves into their dens and lay them down." And yet alike to Indian, panther, and wild-cat, to every oak of the forest, to every foot of land in America, from the stormy Atlantic to the broad Pacific, that day was a day of days.

There had been stormy and windy weather, but now dawned on the earth one of those still, golden times of November, full of dreamy rest and tender calm. The skies above were blue and fair, and the waters of the curving bay were a downward sky—a magical under-world, wherein the crimson oaks, and the dusk plumage of the pine, and the red holly-berries, and yellow sassafras leaves, all flickered and glinted in wavering bands of color as soft winds swayed the glassy floor of waters.

In a moment, there is heard in the silent bay a sound of a rush and ripple, different from the lap of the many-tongued waves on the shore; and, silently as a cloud, with white wings spread, a little vessel glides into the harbor.

A little craft is she—not larger than the fishing-smacks that ply their course along our coasts in summer; but her decks are crowded with men, women, and children, looking out with joyous curiosity on the beautiful bay, where, after many dangers and storms, they first have found safe shelter and hopeful harbor. That small, unknown ship was the *Mayflower*; those men and women who crowded her decks were that little handful of God's own wheat which had been flailed by adversity, tossed and winnowed till every husk of earthly selfishness and self-will had been beaten away from them and left only pure seed, fit for the planting of a new world. It was old Master Cotton Mather who said of them, "The Lord sifted three countries to find seed wherewith to plant America."

Hark now to the hearty cry of the sailors, as with a plash and a cheer the anchor goes down, just in the deep water inside of Long Point; and then, says their journal, "being now passed the vast ocean and sea of troubles, before their preparation unto further proceedings as to seek out a place for habitation, they fell down on their knees and blessed the Lord, the God of heaven, who had brought them over the vast and furious ocean, and delivered them from all perils and miseries thereof."

Let us draw nigh and mingle with this singular act of worship. Elder Brewster, with his well-worn Geneva Bible in hand, leads the thanksgiving in words which, though thousands of years old, seem as if written for the occasion of that hour:

"Praise the Lord because he is good, for his mercy endureth for ever. Let them which have been redeemed of the Lord show how he delivereth them from the hand of the oppressor. And gathered them out of the lands: from the east, and from the west, from the north, and from the south, when they wandered in deserts and wildernesses out of the way and found no city to dwell in. Both hungry and thirsty, their soul failed in them. Then they cried unto the Lord in their troubles, and he delivered them in their distresses. And led them forth by the right way, that they might go unto a city of habitation. They that go down to the sea and occupy by the great waters: they see the works of the Lord and his wonders in the deep. For he commandeth and raiseth the stormy wind, and it lifteth up the waves thereof. They mount up to heaven, and descend to the deep: so that their soul melteth for trouble. They are tossed to and fro, and stagger like a drunken man, and all their cunning is gone. Then they cry unto the Lord in their trouble, and he bringeth them out of their distresses. He turneth the storm to a calm, so that the waves thereof are still. When they are quieted they are glad, and he bringeth them unto the haven where they would be."

As yet, the treasures of sacred song which are the liturgy of modern Christians had not arisen in the church. There was no Watts, and no Wesley, in the days of the Pilgrims; they brought with them in each family, as the most precious of household possessions, a thick volume containing, first, the Book of Common

Prayer, with the Psalter appointed to be read in churches; second, the whole Bible in the Geneva translation, which was the basis on which our present English translation was made; and, third, the Psalms of David, in meter, by Sternhold and Hopkins, with the music notes of the tunes, adapted to singing. Therefore it was that our little band were able to lift up their voices together in song and that the noble tones of Old Hundred for the first time floated over the silent bay and mingled with the sound of winds and waters, consecrating our American shores.

"All people that on earth do dwell,
  Sing to the Lord with cheerful voice:
Him serve with fear, His praise forthtell;
  Come ye before Him and rejoice.

"The Lord, ye know, is God indeed;
  Without our aid He did us make;
We are His flock, He doth us feed,
  And for his sheep He doth us take.

"O enter then His gates with praise,
  Approach with joy His courts unto:
Praise, laud, and bless His name always,
  For it is seemly so to do.

"For why? The Lord our God is good,
  His mercy is forever sure;
His truth at all times firmly stood,
  And shall from age to age endure."

This grand hymn rose and swelled and vibrated in the still November air; while in between the pauses came the warble of birds, the scream of the jay, the hoarse call of hawk and eagle, going on with their forest ways all unmindful of the new era which had been ushered in with those solemn sounds.

Chapter II

The First Day on Shore

THE sound of prayer and psalm-singing died away on the shore, and the little band, rising from their knees, saluted each other in that genial humor which always possesses a ship's company when they have weathered the ocean and come to land together.

"Well, Master Jones, here we are," said Elder Brewster cheerily to the ship-master.

"Aye, aye, sir, here we be sure enough; but I've had many a shrewd doubt of this upshot. I tell you, sirs, when that beam amidships sprung and cracked Master Coppin here said we must give over—hands couldn't bring her through. Thou rememberest, Master Coppin?"

"That I do," replied Master Coppin, the first mate, a stocky, cheery sailor, with a face red and shining as a glazed bun. "I said then that praying might save her, perhaps, but nothing else would."

"Praying wouldn't have saved her," said Master Brown, the carpenter, "if I had not put in that screw and worked the beam to her place again."

"Aye, aye, Master Carpenter," said Elder Brewster, "the Lord hath abundance of the needful ever to his hand. When He wills to answer prayer, there will be found both carpenter and screws in their season, I trow."

"Well, Deb," said Master Coppin, pinching the ear of a great mastiff bitch who sat by him, "what sayest thou? Give us thy mind on it, old girl; say, wilt thou go deer-hunting with us yonder?"

The dog, who was full of the excitement of all around, wagged her tail and gave three tremendous barks, whereat a little spaniel with curly ears, that stood by Rose Standish, barked aloud.

"Well done!" said Captain Miles Standish. "Why, here is a salute of ordnance! Old Deb is in the spirit of the thing and opens out like a cannon. The old girl is spoiling for a chase in those woods."

"Father, may I go ashore? I want to see the country," said Wrestling Brewster, a bright, sturdy boy, creeping up to Elder Brewster and touching his father's elbow.

Thereat there was a crying to the different mothers of girls and boys tired of being cooped up,— "Oh, mother, mother, ask that we may all go ashore."

"For my part," said old Margery the serving-maid to Elder Brewster, "I want to go ashore to wash and be decent, for there isn't a soul of us hath anything fit for Christians. There be springs of water, I trow."

"Never doubt it, my woman," said Elder Brewster; but all things in their order. How say you, Mr. Carver? You are our governor. What order shall we take?"

"We must have up the shallop," said Carver, "and send a picked company to see what entertainment there may be for us on shore."

"And I counsel that all go well armed," quoth Captain Miles Standish, "for these men of the forest are sharper than a thorn-hedge. What! what!" he said, looking over to the eager group of girls and boys, "ye would go ashore, would ye? Why, the lions and bears will make one mouthful of ye."

"I'm not afraid of lions," said young Wrestling Brewster in an aside to little Love Winslow, a golden-haired, pale-cheeked child, of a tender and spiritual beauty of face. "I'd like to meet a lion," he added, "and serve him as Samson did. I'd get honey out of him, I promise."

"Oh, there you are, young Master Boastful!" said old Margery. "Mind the old saying, 'Brag is a good dog, but hold-fast is better.'"

"Dear husband," said Rose Standish, "wilt thou go ashore in this company?"

"Why, aye, sweetheart, what else am I come for—and who should go if not I?"

"Thou art so very venturesome, Miles."

"Even so, my Rose of the wilderness. Why else am I come on this quest? Not being good enough to be in your church nor one of the saints, I come for an arm of flesh to them, and so, here goes on my armor."

And as he spoke, he buried his frank, good-natured countenance in an iron headpiece, and Rose hastened to help him adjust his corselet.

The clang of armor, the bustle and motion of men and children, the barking of dogs, and the cheery Heave-o! of the sailors marked the setting off of the party which comprised some of the gravest, and wisest, as well as the youngest and most able-bodied of the ship's company. The impatient children ran in a group and clustered on the side of the ship to see them go. Old Deb, with her two half-grown pups, barked and yelped after her master in the boat, running up and down the vessel's deck with piteous cries of impatience.

"Come hither, dear old Deb," said little Love Winslow, running up and throwing her arms round the dog's rough neck; "thou must not take on so; thy master will be back again; so be a good dog now, and lie down."

And the great rough mastiff quieted down under her caresses, and sitting down by her she patted and played with her, with her little thin hands.

"See the darling," said Rose Standish, "what a way that baby hath! In all the roughness and the terrors of the sea she hath been like a little sunbeam to us—yet she is so frail!"

"She hath been marked in the womb by the troubles her mother bore," said old Margery, shaking her head. "She never had the ways of other babies, but hath ever that wistful look—and her eyes are brighter than they should be. Mistress Winslow will never raise that child—now mark me!"

"Take care!" said Rose, "let not her mother hear you."

"Why, look at her beside of Wrestling Brewster, or Faith Carver. They are flesh and blood, and she looks as if she had been made out of sunshine. 'Tis a sweet babe as ever was; but fitter for the kingdom of heaven than our rough life—deary me! a hard time we have had of it. I suppose it's all best, but I don't know."

"Oh, never talk that way, Margery," said Rose Standish; "we must all keep up heart, our own and one another's."

"Ah, well a day—I suppose so, but then I look at my good Master Brewster and remember how, when I was a girl, he was at our good Queen Elizabeth's court, ruffling it with the best, and everybody said that there wasn't a young man that had good fortune to equal his. Why, Master Davidson, the Queen's Secretary of State, thought all the world of him; and when he went to Holland on the Queen's business, he must take him along; and when he took the keys of the cities there, it was my master that he trusted them to, who used to sleep with them under his pillow. I remember when he came home to the Queen's court, wearing the great gold chain that the States had given him. Ah me! I little thought he would ever come to a poor man's coat, then!"

"Well, good Margery," said Rose, "it isn't the coat, but the heart under it—that's the thing. Thou hast more cause of pride in thy master's poverty than in his riches."

"May be so—I don't know," said Margery, "but he hath had many a sore trouble in worldly things—driven and hunted from place to place in England, clapt into prison, and all he had eaten up with fines and charges and costs."

"All that is because he chose rather to suffer affliction with the people of God than to enjoy the pleasures of sin for a season," said Rose; "he shall have his reward by and by."

"Well, there be good men and godly in Old England that get to heaven in better coats and with easy carriages and fine houses and servants, and I would my master had been of such. But if he must come to the wilderness I will come with him. Gracious me! what noise is that?" she exclaimed, as a sudden report of firearms from below struck her ear. "I do believe there is that Frank Billington at the gunpowder; that boy will never leave, I do believe, till he hath blown up the ship's company."

In fact, it appeared that young master Frank, impatient of the absence of his father, had toled Wrestling Brewster and two other of the boys down into the cabin to show them his skill in managing his father's fowling-piece, had burst the gun, scattering the pieces about the cabin.

Margery soon appeared, dragging the culprit after her. "Look here now, Master Malapert, see what you'll get when your father comes home! Lord a mercy! here was half a keg of powder standing open! Enough to have blown us all up! Here, Master Clarke, Master Clarke, come and keep this boy with you till his father come back, or we be all sent sky high before we know."

At even tide the boat came back laden to the water's edge with the first gettings and givings from the new soil of America. There is a richness and sweetness gleaming through the brief records of these men in their journals, which shows how the new land was seen through a fond and tender medium, half poetic; and its new products lend a savor to them of somewhat foreign and rare.

Of this day's expedition the record is thus:

"That day, so soon as we could, we set ashore some fifteen or sixteen men well armed, with some to fetch wood, for we had none left; as also to see what the land was and what inhabitants they could meet with. They found it to be a small neck of land on this side where we lay in the bay, and on the further side the sea, the ground or earth, sand-hills, much like the downs in Holland, but much better; the crust of the earth a spit's depth of excellent black earth; all wooded with oaks, pines, sassafras, juniper, birch, holly, vines, some ash and walnut; the wood for the most part open and without underwood, fit either to walk or to ride in. At night our people returned and found not any people or inhabitants, and laded their boat with juniper, which smelled very sweet and strong, and of which we burned for the most part while we were there."

"See there," said little Love Winslow, "what fine red berries Captain Miles Standish hath brought."

"Yea, my little maid, there is a brave lot of holly berries for thee to dress the cabin withal. We shall not want for Christmas greens here, though the houses and churches are yet to come."

"Yea, Brother Miles" said Elder Brewster, "the trees of the Lord are full of sap in this land, even the cedars of Lebanon, which he hath planted. It hath the look to me of a land which the Lord our God hath blessed."

"There is a most excellent depth of black, rich earth," said Carver, "and a great tangle of grapevines, whereon the leaves in many places yet hung, and we picked up stores of walnuts under a tree—not so big as our English ones—but sweet and well-flavored."

"Know ye, brethren, what in this land smelleth sweetest to me?" said Elder Brewster. "It is the smell of liberty. The soil is free—no man hath claim thereon. In Old England a poor man may starve right on his mother's bosom; there may be stores of fish in the river, and bird and fowl flying, and deer running by, and yet though a man's children be crying for bread, an' he catch a fish or snare a bird, he shall be snatched up and hanged. This is a sore evil in Old England; but we will make a country here for the poor to dwell in, where the wild fruits and fish and fowl shall be the inheritance of whosoever will have them; and every man shall have his portion of our good mother earth, with no lords and no bishops to harry and distrain, and worry with taxes and tythes."

"Amen, brother!" said Miles Standish, "and thereto I give my best endeavors with sword and buckler."

Chapter III

Christmas Tide in Plymouth Harbor

FOR the rest of that month of November the *Mayflower* lay at anchor in Cape Cod harbor, and formed a floating home for the women and children, while the men were out exploring the country, with a careful and steady shrewdness and good sense, to determine where should be the site of the future colony. The record of their adventures is given in their journals with that sweet homeliness of phrase which hangs about the Old English of that period like the smell of rosemary in an ancient cabinet.

We are told of a sort of picnic day, when "our women went on shore to wash and all to refresh themselves;" and fancy the times there must have been among the little company, while the mothers sorted and washed and dried the linen, and the children, under the keeping of the old mastiffs and with many cautions against the wolves and wild cubs, once more had liberty to play in the green wood. For it appears in these journals how, in one case, the little spaniel of John Goodman was chased by two wolves, and was fain to take refuge between his master's legs for shelter. Goodman "had nothing in hand," says the journal, "but took up a stick and threw at one of them and hit him, and they presently ran away, but came again. He got a pale-board in his hand, but they both sat on their tails a good while, grinning at him, and then went their way and left him."

Such little touches show what the care of families must have been in the woodland picnics, and why the ship was, on the whole, the safest refuge for the women and children.

We are told, moreover, how the party who had struck off into the wilderness, "having marched through boughs and bushes and under hills and valleys which tore our very armor in pieces, yet could meet with no inhabitants nor find any fresh water which we greatly stood in need of, for we brought neither beer nor water with us, and our victual was only biscuit and Holland cheese, and a little bottle of aqua vitae. So we were sore athirst. About ten o'clock we came into a deep valley full of brush, sweet gaile and long grass, through which we found little paths or tracks; and we saw there a deer and found springs of water, of which we were heartily glad, and sat us down and drunk our first New England water with as much delight as we ever drunk drink in all our lives."

Three such expeditions through the country, with all sorts of haps and mishaps and adventures, took up the time until near the 15th of December, when, having selected a spot for their colony, they weighed anchor to go to their future home.

Plymouth Harbor, as they found it, is thus described:

"This harbor is a bay greater than Cape Cod, compassed with a goodly land, and in the bay two fine islands uninhabited, wherein are nothing but woods, oaks, pines, walnuts, beeches, sassafras, vines, and other trees which we know not. The bay is a most hopeful place, innumerable stores of fowl, and excellent good; and it cannot but be of fish in their season. Skate, cod, and turbot, and herring we have tasted of—abundance of mussels (clams) the best we ever saw; and crabs and lobsters in their time, infinite."

On the main land they write:

"The land is, for a spit's depth, excellent black mould and fat in some places. Two or three great oaks, pines, walnut, beech, ash, birch, hazel, holly, and sassafras in abundance, and vines every-where, with cherry-trees, plum-trees, and others which we know not. Many kind of herbs we found here in winter, as strawberry leaves innumerable, sorrel, yarrow, carvel, brook-lime, liver-wort, watercresses, with great store of leeks and onions, and an excellent strong kind of flax and hemp."

It is evident from this description that the season was a mild one even thus late into December, that there was still sufficient foliage hanging upon the trees to determine the species, and that the pilgrims viewed their new mother-land through eyes of cheerful hope.

And now let us look in the glass at them once more, on Saturday morning of the 23d of December.

The little *Mayflower* lies swinging at her moorings in the harbor, while every man and boy who could use a tool has gone on shore to cut down and prepare timber for future houses.

Mary Winslow and Rose Standish are sitting together on deck, fashioning garments, while little Love Winslow is playing at their feet with such toys as the new world afforded her—strings of acorns and scarlet holly-berries and some bird-claws and arrowheads and bright-colored ears of Indian corn, which Captain Miles Standish has brought home to her from one of their explorations.

Through the still autumnal air may now and then be heard the voices of men calling to one another on shore, the quick, sharp ring of axes, and anon the crash of falling trees, with shouts from juveniles as the great forest monarch is laid low. Some of the women are busy below, sorting over and arranging their little household stores and stuff with a view to moving on shore, and holding domestic consultations with each other.

A sadness hangs over the little company, for since their arrival the stroke of death has more than once fallen; we find in Bradford's brief record that by the 24th of December six had died.

What came nearest to the hearts of all was the loss of Dorothea Bradford, who, when all the men of the party were absent on an exploring tour, accidentally fell over the side of the vessel and sunk in the deep waters. What this loss was to the husband and the little company of brothers and sisters appears by no note or word of wailing, merely by a simple entry which says no more than the record on a gravestone, that, "on the 7th of December, Dorothy, wife of William Bradford, fell over and was drowned."

That much-enduring company could afford themselves few tears. Earthly having and enjoying was a thing long since dismissed from their calculations. They were living on the primitive Christian platform; they "rejoiced as though they rejoiced not," and they "wept as though they wept not," and they "had wives and children as though they had them not," or, as one of themselves expressed it, "We are in all places strangers, pilgrims, travelers and sojourners; our dwelling is but a wandering, our abiding but as a fleeting, our home is nowhere but in the heavens, in that house not made with hands, whose builder and maker is God."

When one of their number fell they were forced to do as soldiers in the stress of battle—close up the ranks and press on.

But Mary Winslow, as she sat over her sewing, dropped now and then a tear down on her work for the loss of her sister and counselor and long-tried friend. From the lower part of the ship floated up, at intervals, snatches of an old English ditty that Margery was singing while she moved to and fro about her work, one of those genuine English melodies, full of a rich, strange mournfulness blent with a soothing pathos:

"Fear no more the heat o' the sun
    Nor the furious winter rages,
Thou thy worldly task hast done,
    Home art gone and ta'en thy wages."

The air was familiar, and Mary Winslow, dropping her work in her lap, involuntarily joined in it:

"Fear no more the frown of the great,
    Thou art past the tyrant's stroke;
 Care no more to clothe and eat,
    To thee the reed is as the oak."

"There goes a great tree on shore!" quoth little Love Winslow, clapping her hands. "Dost hear, mother? I've been counting the strokes—fifteen—and then crackle! crackle! crackle! and down it comes!"

"Peace, darling," said Mary Winslow; "hear what old Margery is singing below:

"Fear no more the lightning's flash,
    Nor the all-dreaded thunder stone;
 Fear not slander, censure rash—
    Thou hast finished joy and moan.
 All lovers young—all lovers must
    Consign to thee, and come to dust."

"Why do you cry, mother?" said the little one, climbing on her lap and wiping her tears.

"I was thinking of dear Auntie, who is gone from us."

"She is not gone from us, mother."

"My darling, she is with Jesus."

"Well, mother, Jesus is ever with us—you tell me that—and if she is with him she is with us too—I know she is—for sometimes I see her. She sat by me last night and stroked my head when that ugly stormy wind waked me—she looked so sweet, oh, ever so beautiful!—and she made me go to sleep so quiet—it is sweet to be as she is, mother—not away from us but with Jesus."

"These little ones see further in the kingdom than we," said Rose Standish. "If we would be like them, we should take things easier. When the Lord would show who was greatest in his kingdom, he took a little child on his lap."

"Ah me, Rose!" said Mary Winslow, "I am aweary in spirit with this tossing sea-life. I long to have a home on dry land once more, be it ever so poor. The sea wearies me. Only think, it is almost Christmas time, only two days now to Christmas. How shall we keep it in these woods?"

"Aye, aye," said old Margery, coming up at the moment, "a brave muster and to do is there now in old England; and men and boys going forth singing and bearing home branches of holly, and pine, and mistletoe for Christmas greens. Oh! I remember I used to go forth with them and help dress the churches. God help the poor children, they will grow up in the wilderness and never see such brave sights as I have. They will never know what a church is, such as they are in old England, with fine old windows like the clouds, and rainbows, and great wonderful arches like the very skies above us, and the brave music with the old organs rolling and the boys marching in white garments and singing so as should draw the very heart out of one. All this we have left behind in old England—ah! well a day! well a day!"

"Oh, but, Margery," said Mary Winslow, "we have a 'better country' than old England, where the saints and angels are keeping Christmas; we confess that we are strangers and pilgrims on earth."

And Rose Standish immediately added the familiar quotation from the Geneva Bible:

"For they that say such things declare plainly that they seek a country. For if they had been mindful of that country from whence they came out they had leisure to have returned. But now they desire a better—that is, an heavenly; wherefore God is not ashamed of them to be called their God."

The fair young face glowed as she repeated the heroic words, for already, though she knew it not, Rose Standish was feeling the approaching sphere of the angel life. Strong in spirit, as delicate in frame, she had given herself and drawn her martial husband to the support of a great and noble cause; but while the spirit was ready, the flesh was weak, and even at that moment her name was written in the Lamb's Book to enter the higher life in one short month's time from that Christmas.

Only one month of sweetness and perfume was that sweet rose to shed over the hard and troubled life of the pilgrims, for the saints and angels loved her, and were from day to day gently untying mortal bands to draw her to themselves. Yet was there nothing about her of mournfulness; on the contrary, she was ever alert and bright, with a ready tongue to cheer and a helpful hand to do; and, seeing the sadness that seemed stealing over Mary Winslow, she struck another key, and, catching little Love up in her arms, said cheerily, "Come hither, pretty one, and Rose will sing thee a brave carol for Christmas. We won't be down-hearted, will we? Hark now to what the minstrels used to sing under my window when I was a little girl:

"I saw three ships come sailing in
 On Christmas day, on Christmas day;
 I saw three ships come sailing in
 On Christmas day in the morning.

"And what was in those ships all three
 On Christmas day, on Christmas day;
 And what was in those ships all three
 On Christmas day in the morning ?

"Our Saviour Christ and his laydie,
 On Christmas day, on Christmas day;
 Our Saviour Christ and his laydie
 On Christmas day in the morning.

"Pray, whither sailed those ships all three,
On Christmas day, on Christmas day?
Oh, they sailed into Bethlehem,
On Christmas day in the morning.

"And all the bells on earth shall ring
On Christmas day, on Christmas day;
And all the angels in heaven shall sing
On Christmas day in the morning.

"Then let us all rejoice amain,
 On Christmas day, on Christmas day;
 Then let us all rejoice amain
 On Christmas day in the morning."

"Now, isn't that a brave ballad?" said Rose.

"Yea, and thou singest like a real English robin," said Margery, "to do the heart good to hear thee."

Chapter IV

Elder Brewster's Christmas Sermon

SUNDAY morning found the little company gathered once more on the ship, with nothing to do but rest and remember their homes, temporal and spiritual—homes backward, in old England, and forward, in Heaven. They were, every man and woman of them, English to the back-bone. From Captain Jones who commanded the ship to Elder Brewster who ruled and guided in spiritual affairs, all alike were of that stock and breeding which made the Englishman of the days of Bacon and Shakespeare, and in those days Christmas was knit into the heart of every one of them by a thousand threads, which no after years could untie.

Christmas carols had been sung to them by nurses and mothers and grandmothers; the Christmas holly spoke to them from every berry and prickly leaf, full of dearest household memories. Some of them had been men of substance among the English gentry, and in their prosperous days had held high festival in ancestral halls in the season of good cheer. Elder Brewster himself had been a rising young diplomat in the court of Elizabeth, in the days when the Lord Keeper of the Seals led the revels of Christmas as Lord of Misrule.

So that, though this Sunday morning arose gray and lowering, with snow-flakes hovering through the air, there was Christmas in the thoughts of every man and woman among them—albeit it was the Christmas of wanderers and exiles in a wilderness looking back to bright home-fires across stormy waters.

The men had come back from their work on shore with branches of green pine and holly, and the women had stuck them about the ship, not without tearful thoughts of old home-places, where their childhood fathers and mothers did the same.

Bits and snatches of Christmas carols were floating all around the ship, like land-birds blown far out to sea. In the fore-castle Master Coppin was singing:

> "Come, bring with a noise,
> My merry boys,
>   The Christmas log to the firing;
> While my good dame, she
> Bids ye all be free,
>   And drink to your hearts' desiring.
> Drink now the strong beer,
> Cut the white loaf here.
>   The while the meat is shredding
> For the rare minced pie,
> And the plums stand by
>   To fill the paste that's a-kneading."

"Ah, well-a-day, Master Jones, it is dull cheer to sing Christmas songs here in the woods, with only the owls and the bears for choristers. I wish I could hear the bells of merry England once more."

And down in the cabin Rose Standish was hushing little Peregrine, the first American-born baby, with a Christmas lullaby:

> "This winter's night
> I saw a sight—
>   A star as bright as day;
> And ever among
> A maiden sung,
>   Lullay, by-by, lullay!

"This lovely laydie sat and sung,
  And to her child she said,
My son, my brother, and my father dear,
    Why lyest thou thus in hayd?
My sweet bird,
Tho' it betide
    Thou be not king veray;
But nevertheless
I will not cease
    To sing, by-by, lullay!

"The child then spake in his talking,
    And to his mother he said,
It happeneth, mother, I am a king,
    In crib though I be laid,
For angels bright
Did down alight,
    Thou knowest it is no nay;
And of that sight
Thou may'st be light
    To sing, by-by, lullay!

"Now, sweet son, since thou art a king,
    Why art thou laid in stall?
Why not ordain thy bedding
    In some great king his hall?
We thinketh 'tis right
That king or knight
    Should be in good array;
And them among,
It were no wrong
    To sing, by-by, lullay!

"Mary, mother, I am thy child,
　　Tho' I be laid in stall;
Lords and dukes shall worship me,
　　And so shall kinges all.
And ye shall see
That kinges three
　　Shall come on the twelfth day;
For this behest
Give me thy breast,
　　And sing, by-by, lullay!"

"See here," quoth Miles Standish, "when my Rose singeth, the children gather round her like bees round a flower. Come, let us all strike up a goodly carol together. Sing one, sing all, girls and boys, and get a bit of Old England's Christmas before to-morrow, when we must to our work on shore."

Thereat Rose struck up a familiar ballad-meter of a catching rhythm, and every voice of young and old was soon joining in it:

"Behold a silly,* tender Babe,
　　In freezing winter night,
In homely manger trembling lies;
　　Alas! a piteous sight,
The inns are full, no man will yield
　　This little Pilgrim bed;
But forced He is, with silly beasts
　　In crib to shroud His, head.
Despise Him not for lying there,
　　First what He is inquire:
An orient pearl is often found
　　In depth of dirty mire.

"Weigh not His crib, His wooden dish,
　　Nor beasts that by Him feed;
Weigh not His mother's poor attire,

---

*Old English—simple.

> Nor Joseph's simple weed.
> This stable is a Prince's court,
> The crib His chair of state,
> The beasts are parcel of His pomp,
> The wooden dish His plate.
> The persons in that poor attire
> His royal liveries wear;
> The Prince Himself is come from Heaven,
> This pomp is prized there.
> With joy approach, O Christian wight,
> Do homage to thy King;
> And highly praise His humble pomp,
> Which He from Heaven doth bring."

The cheerful sounds spread themselves through the ship like the flavor of some rare perfume, bringing softness of heart through a thousand tender memories.

Anon, the hour of Sabbath morning worship drew on, and Elder Brewster read from the New Testament the whole story of the Nativity, and then gave a sort of Christmas homily from the words of St. Paul, in the eighth chapter of Romans, the sixth and seventh verses, which the Geneva version thus renders:

"For the wisdom of the flesh is death, but the wisdom of the spirit is life and peace.

For the wisdom of the flesh is enmity against God, for it is not subject to the law of God, neither indeed can be."

"Ye know full well, dear brethren, what the wisdom of the flesh sayeth. The wisdom of the flesh sayeth to each one, 'Take care of thyself; look after thyself, to get and to have and to hold and to enjoy.' The wisdom of the flesh sayeth, 'So thou art warm, full, and in good liking, take thine ease, eat, drink, and be merry, and care not how many go empty and be lacking.' But ye have seen in the Gospel this morning that this was not the wisdom of our Lord Jesus Christ, who, though he was Lord of all, became poorer than any, that we, through His poverty, might become rich. When our Lord Jesus Christ came, the wisdom of the flesh despised Him; the wisdom of the flesh had no room for Him at the inn.

"There was room enough always for Herod and his concubines, for the wisdom of the flesh set great store by them; but a poor man and woman were thrust out to a stable; and *there* was a poor baby born whom the wisdom of the flesh knew not, because the wisdom of the flesh is enmity against God.

"The wisdom of the flesh, brethren, ever despiseth the wisdom of God, because it knoweth it not. The wisdom of the flesh looketh at the thing that is great and strong and high ; it looketh at riches, at kings' courts, at fine clothes and fine jewels and fine feastings, and it despiseth the little and the poor and the weak.

"But the wisdom of the Spirit goeth to worship the poor babe in the manger, and layeth gold and myrrh and frankincense at his feet while he lieth in weakness and poverty, as did the wise men who were taught of God.

"Now, forasmuch as our Saviour Christ left His riches and throne in glory and came in weakness and poverty to this world, that he might work out a mighty salvation that shall be to all people, how can we better keep Christmas than to follow in his steps? We be a little company who have forsaken houses and lands and possessions, and come here unto the wilderness that we may prepare a resting-place whereto others shall come to reap what we shall sow. And to-morrow we shall keep our first Christmas, not in flesh-pleasing and in reveling and in fullness of bread, but in small beginning and great weakness, as our Lord Christ kept it when He was born in a stable and lay in a manger.

"To-morrow, God willing, we will all go forth to do good, honest Christian work, and begin the first house-building in this our New England—it may be roughly fashioned, but as good a house, I'll warrant me, as our Lord Christ had on the Christmas Day we wot of. And let us not faint in heart because the wisdom of the world despiseth what we do. Though Sanballat the Horonite, and Tobias the Ammonite, and Geshem the Arabian make scorn of us, and say, 'What do these weak Jews? If a fox go up, he shall break down their stone wall;' yet the Lord our God is with us, and He can cause our work to prosper.

"The wisdom of the Spirit seeth the grain of mustard-seed, that is the least of all seeds, how it shall become a great tree, and the fowls of heaven shall lodge in its branches. Let us, then, lift up the hands that hang down and the feeble knees, and let us hope that, like as great salvation to all people came out of small beginnings of Bethlehem, so the work which we shall begin to-morrow shall be for the good of many nations.

"It is a custom on this Christmas Day to give love-presents. What love-gift giveth our Lord Jesus on this day? Brethren, it is a great one and a precious; as St. Paul said to the Philippians: 'For unto you it is given for Christ, not only that ye should believe on Him, but also that ye should *suffer* for His sake;' and St. Peter also saith, 'Behold, we count them blessed which endure.' And the holy Apostles rejoiced that they were counted worthy to suffer rebuke for the name of Jesus.

"Our Lord Christ giveth us of His cup and His baptism; He giveth of the manger and the straw; He giveth of persecutions and afflictions; He giveth of the crown of thorns, and right dear unto us be these gifts.

"And now will I tell these children a story, which a cunning playwright, whom I once knew in our Queen's court, hath made concerning gifts:

"A great king would marry his daughter worthily, and so he caused three caskets to be made, in one of which he hid her picture. The one casket was of gold set with diamonds, the second of silver set with pearls, and the third a poor casket of lead.

"Now it was given out that each comer should have but one choice, and if he chose the one with the picture he should have the lady to wife.

"Divers kings, knights, and gentlemen came from far, but they never won, because they always snatched at the gold and the silver caskets, with the pearls and diamonds, So, when they opened these, they found only a grinning death's-head or a fool's cap.

"But anon cometh a true, brave knight and gentleman, who chooseth for love alone the old leaden casket; and, behold, within is the picture of her he loveth! and they were married with great feasting and content.

"So our Lord Jesus doth not offer himself to us in silver and gold and jewels, but in poverty and hardness and want; but whoso chooseth them for His love's sake shall find Him therein whom his soul loveth, and shall enter with joy to the marriage supper of the Lamb.

"And when the Lord shall come again in his glory, then he shall bring worthy gifts with him, for he saith: 'Be thou faithful unto death, and I will give thee a crown of life; to him that overcometh I will give to eat of the hidden manna, and I will give him a white stone with a new name that no man knoweth save he that receiveth it. He that overcometh and keepeth my words, I will give power over the nations and I will give him the morning star.'

"Let us then take joyfully Christ's Christmas gifts of labors and adversities and crosses to-day, that when he shall appear we may have these great and wonderful gifts at his coming; for if we suffer with him we shall also reign; but if we deny him, he also will deny us."

And so it happens that the only record of Christmas Day in the pilgrims' journal is this:

"Monday, the 25th, being Christmas Day, we went ashore, some to fell timber, some to saw, some to rive, and some to carry; and so no man rested all that day. But towards night some, as they were at work, heard a noise of Indians, which caused us all to go to our muskets; but we heard no further, so we came aboard again, leaving some to keep guard. That night we had a sore storm of wind and rain. But at night the ship-master caused us to have some beer aboard."

So worthily kept they the first Christmas, from which comes all the Christmas cheer of New England to-day. There is no record how Mary Winslow and Rose Standish and others, with women and children, came ashore and walked about encouraging the builders; and how little Love gathered stores of bright cbecker-berries and partridge plums, and was made merry in seeing squirrels and wild rabbits; nor how old Margery roasted certain wild geese to a turn at a woodland fire, and con-served wild cranberries with honey for sauce. In their journals the good pilgrims say they found bushels of strawberries in the meadows in December. But we, knowing the nature of things, know that these must have been cranberries, which grow still abundantly around Plymouth harbor.

And at the very time that all this was doing in the wilder-ness, and the men were working yeomanly to build a new nation, in King James's court the ambassadors of the French King were being entertained with maskings and mummerings, wherein the staple subject of merriment was the Puritans!

So goes the wisdom of the world and its ways—and so goes the wisdom of God!